Relax and enjoy!

Kumon's First Steps Workbooks are designed so that children and parents can learn and have fun together. Children learn best from active and participatory parents, so please help your child with the activities in this book. By helping, you are encouraging your child to develop a desire to learn, as well as laying the foundation for him or her to become a self-motivated learner.

How to choose glue and how to paste

If your child will be using glue for the first time, carefully select a type of glue that he or she will enjoy using.

Please choose a child-safe product in an easy-to-use container. Your child can use a glue stick but it is best for children to use glue that can be applied by hand. Children enjoy the tactile experience of spreading glue with their fingers.

▲ Please choose child-safe glue.

Tips for pasting

Line your table with scrap paper before your child starts. Have your child apply an appropriate amount of glue onto the tip of his or her middle finger and then spread it thinly on the part to be pasted. Please put the glue on the side with the glue symbol. When your child is applying glue, encourage him or her to hold the part with one hand and apply the glue onto it with the other. This is difficult for young children, so you can hold the paper for your child at first.

▲ Begin by placing glue onto the part. Then ask your child to use his or her finger to spread the glue on the designated area.

D1497263

How to paste

Your child may already be familiar with playing with stickers, but perhaps he or she is used to just pasting them randomly. It may be difficult at first for your child to paste stickers onto a specific place, but be patient. In time, your child will master this skill.

It does not matter if your child cannot paste accurately or if the image he or she has created is not perfect. He or she will gradually learn to paste parts onto designated areas.

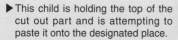

When your child is first attempting to paste a part onto a background, encourage him or her to place the edges down first and then slowly press the rest of the part into place. Your child will gradually learn how to align the parts correctly.

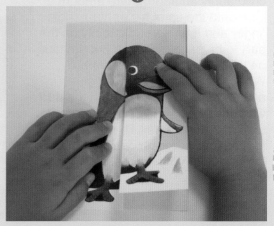

▶ This child is holding the top of the cut out part and is attempting to paste it onto the designated place.

To be used in 3 .

To be used in 4 (lion).

To be used in 5 (bird).

To be used in 6 (whale) .

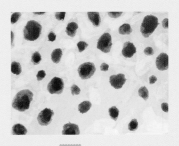

To be used in 8 (cheetah).

3 Aquarium

To parents
Please remove the second sheet of stickers and give it to your child. This sheet is to be used with exercises 3, 4, 5, 6 and 8. On this page, your child will practice pasting stickers wherever he or she would like. When your child has completed the activity, say "aquarium" aloud while pointing to the word.

Example

Paste the stickers as you like.

aquarium

4 Lion

Done!

To parents
In the next series of exercises, your child will paste a sticker that corresponds to the shape of the white area on the page. Since the sticker for this page is round, your child will not have to worry about the sticker's orientation when placing it on the white area.

Paste the sticker onto the lion.

lion

5 **Bird**

Done!

Paste the sticker onto the bird.

bird

6 **Whale Spout**

Done!

Paste the sticker onto the whale.

whale

7 Squid

Done!

To parents
On this page, your child will paste a triangular sticker. Your child should pay attention to the orientation of the sticker because this triangle does not have 3 equal sides. Do not be concerned if the sticker is slightly off the white area. If he or she has successfully chosen the correct orientation, offer lots of praise.

Paste the sticker onto the squid.

squid

8 **Cheetah**

Done!

To parents
This is the last activity in which your child will use stickers. On this page, the orientation of the sticker is important. If your child is having difficulty knowing where to place the sticker, point out the pattern of the cheetah as a hint.

Paste the sticker onto the cheetah.

cheetah

9 **Octopus Band**

Done!

To parents
From this page on, your child will practice pasting with glue. In the beginning, you can put glue on the back of the cut out part for your child. When your child has completed the exercise, say "octopus" aloud while pointing to the word.

Paste the cut out part onto the octopus. octopus

✂ Parents: Please cut this part out for your child. →

Done!

To parents
Your child will paste a circular part on this page. When your child has completed the exercise, say "ladybug" aloud while pointing to the word.

Paste the cut out part onto the ladybug.   ladybug

✂ Parents: Please cut this part out for your child. ➡

Done!

To parents
The cow has a pattern on it, but do not be concerned if the cut out piece is not placed perfectly onto the picture. The most important thing is that your child enjoys pasting with glue.

Paste the cut out part onto the cow.   COW

✂ Parents: Please cut this part out for your child. ➜

12 Zebra Stripes

Done!

Paste the cut out part onto the zebra.

zebra

✂ Parents: Please cut this part out for your child.

13 **Raccoon**

Done!

To parents
The white area in this exercise is designed to be smaller than the cut out part so that no white will show when your child pastes the part on top of it.

Paste the cut out part onto the raccoon.   raccoon

← ✂ Parents: Please cut this part out for your child.

Done!

Paste the cut out part onto the firefly.

firefly

← ✂ Parents: Please cut this part out for your child.

Bear Handstand

To parents
Animal faces are familiar to children, so it should be relatively easy for your child to decide how to glue the cut out part.

Paste the cut out part onto the bear's face.

bear

✂ Parents: Please cut this part out for your child. ↑

Done!

Paste the cut out part onto the hippopotamus' face.

hippopotamus

✂ Parents: Please cut this part out for your child. ↑

17 **Crocodile**

To parents
Have your child hold the cut out part with one dry hand and spread the glue with the other hand. When he or she has completed the exercise, offer lots of praise.

Paste the cut out part onto the crocodile's face.

crocodile

✂ Parents: Please cut this part out for your child. ↑

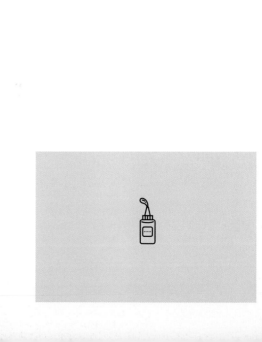

18 Hedgehog

Done!

Paste the cut out part onto the hedgehog's face.

hedgehog

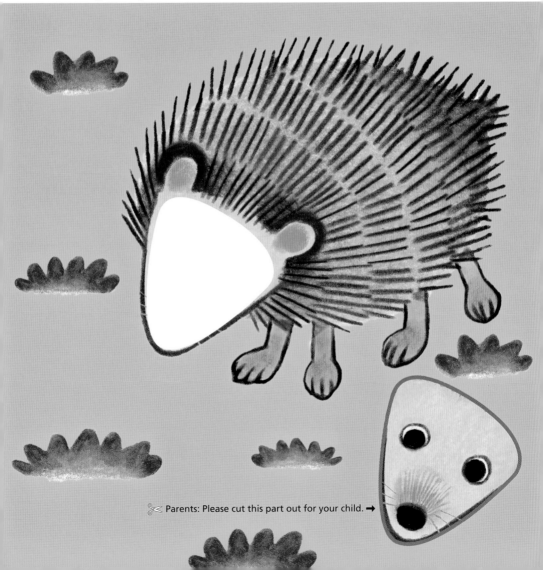

✂ Parents: Please cut this part out for your child. ➡

19 Flying Squirrel

Done!

To parents
Before your child starts pasting, encourage him or her to look carefully at
the sample on the right and the shape of the white area. When he or she
is finished, offer lots of praise.

Paste the cut out part onto the flying squirrel.

flying squirrel

✂ Parents: Please cut this part out for your child. ➜

Mommy and Little Piggy

Done!

To parents
Pasting small parts of paper is not easy for young children. It's okay if the cut out parts are not completely aligned with the white areas. When your child has completed the exercise, offer lots of praise.

Paste the cut out parts onto the pig.

pig

✂ Parents: Please cut these parts out for your child.

21 Snails in the Rain

Example

To parents
Your child can paste the cut out parts wherever he or she pleases. Encourage your child to be creative.

Paste the snails as you like.

snail

✂ Parents: Please cut these parts out for your child.

Done!

Paste the cut out part onto the kangaroo.

kangaroo

✂ Parents: Please cut this part out for your child. ➡

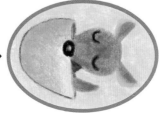

Done!

To parents
The white area is designed to be smaller than the cut out part so that no white will show when your child pastes the part on top of it.

Paste the cut out part onto the cat.

cat

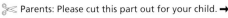 Parents: Please cut this part out for your child. →

24 Cuddling Koalas

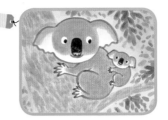

To parents
Before your child starts pasting, encourage him or her to look carefully at the sample on the right and the shape of the white area.

Paste the cut out part onto the koala.   koala

✂ Parents: Please cut this part out for your child. ➜

25 Beetle

Done!

Paste the cut out part onto the beetle.

beetle

✂ Parents: Please cut this part out for your child. ➡

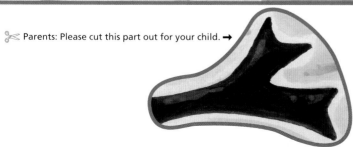

26 Glacier

Example

Paste the animals as you like.

glacier

✂ Parents: Please cut these parts out for your child.

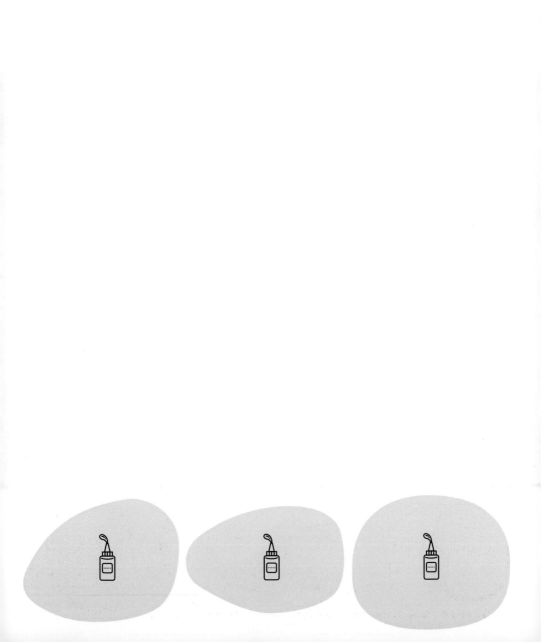

27 Insect Collecting

Example

To parents
Don't be concerned if the image your child has created is not perfect. When he or she has finished the activity, say something like, "Which insect do you like the most?"

Paste the insects as you like.

insect

✁ Parents: Please cut these parts out for your child.

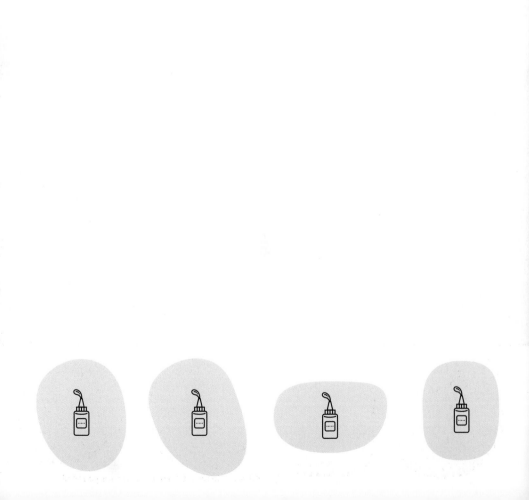

28 Safari Park

To parents
When your child is finished, offer lots of praise and say something like,
"Well done!" or "Would you like to go on a safari?"

Paste the animals as you like.

safari

✂ Parents: Please cut these parts out for your child.

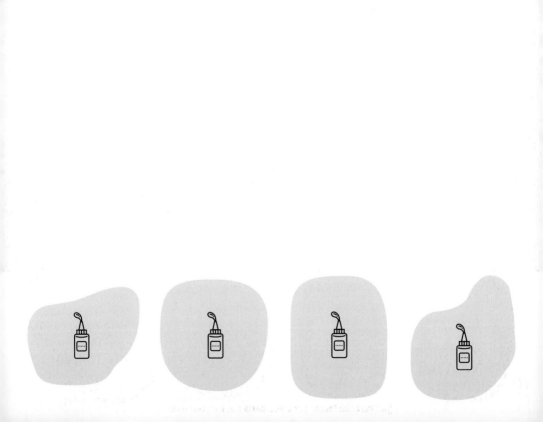

Monkey Playground

Example

To parents
Pasting small parts is not easy for young children. When your child has completed the exercise, offer lots of praise and say something like, "Well done!" or "What are the monkeys doing?"

Paste the monkeys as you like.

monkey

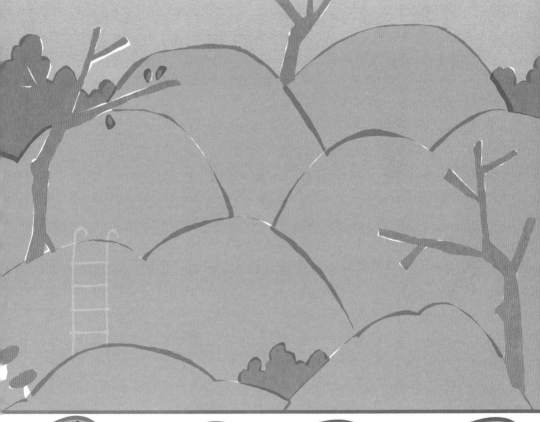

✂ Parents: Please cut these parts out for your child.

Paste the cut out part onto the white area to complete the penguin.

✂ Parents: Please cut along ▬▬▬ for your child.

penguin

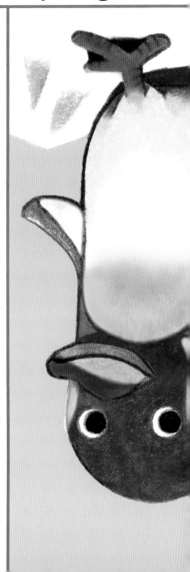

Done!

To parents
Encourage your child to try to figure out how to join the parts of the dog together without your help.

Paste the cut out parts onto the white area to complete the dog.

✂ Parents: Please cut along ▬▬▬ for your child.

dog

Done!

To parents
Before using glue, tell your child to place the cut out parts onto the white area to see which way they should go.

Paste the cut out parts onto the white area to complete the fox.

fox

✂ Parents: Please cut along ▬▬▬ for your child.

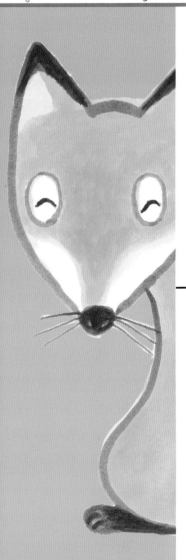

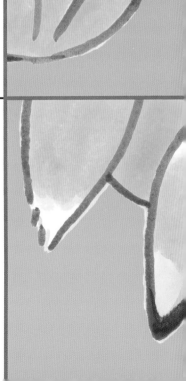

33 Rabbit

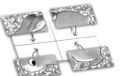

To parents
Encourage your child to place the parts several different ways before pasting them with glue. When he or she is finished, offer lots of praise and say something like, "Well done! That's cute."

Paste the cut out parts onto the white area to complete the rabbit.

✂ Parents: Please cut along ▬▬▬ for your child.

rabbit

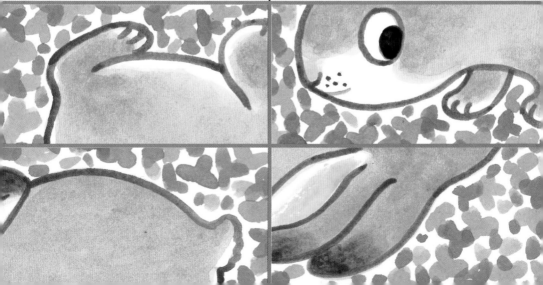

To parents

It's okay if your child has pasted a part in the wrong direction or in the wrong place. It's more important that your child enjoys pasting.

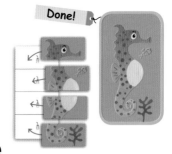

Done!

Paste the cut out parts onto the white area to complete the sea horse.

✂ Parents: Please cut along ▬▬▬ for your child.

sea horse

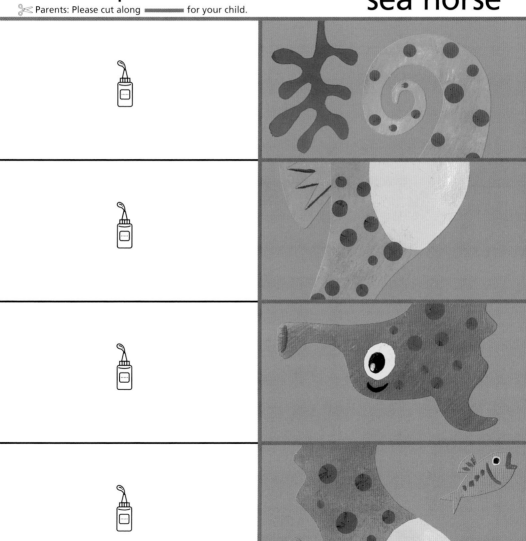

Wild Boar Family

Done!

Paste the cut out parts onto the white area to complete the wild boar family.

wild boar

✂ Parents: Please cut along ▬▬▬ for your child.

36 Crane

Done!

To parents
From this page forward, your child will arrange and paste 6 pieces of an illustration. Don't be concerned if the image that your child creates is not perfect.

Paste the cut out parts onto the white area to complete the crane.

✂ Parents: Please cut along ▬▬▬ for your child.

crane

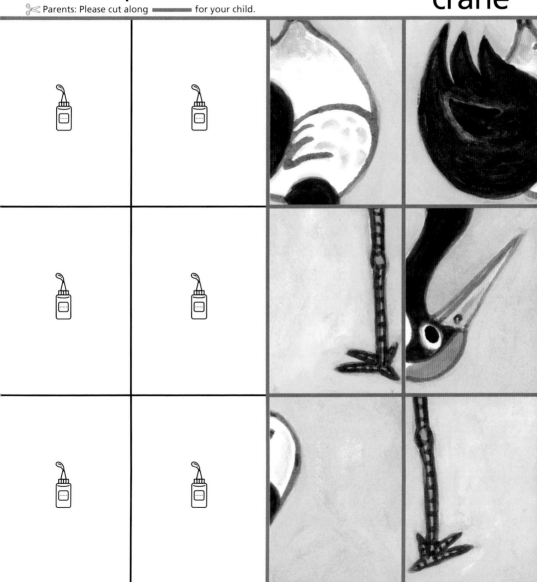

To parents
It may be a good idea to place the cut out parts onto the illustration to check their placement before using glue. Encourage your child to figure out how to create the picture from the 6 pieces.

Paste the cut out parts onto the white area to complete the giraffe.

giraffe

✂ Parents: Please cut along ▬▬▬▬ for your child.

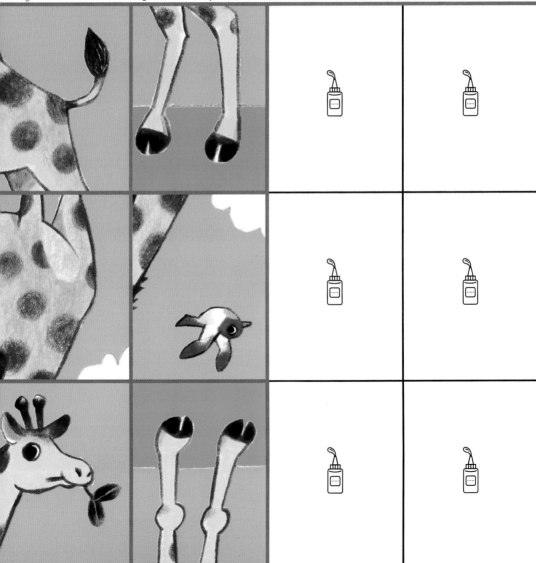

Dashing Dachshund

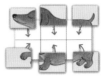

Done!

To parents
If your child seems to be having difficulty, offer to help. When your child has finished, offer lots of praise.

Paste the cut out parts onto the white area to complete the dachshund.

✂ Parents: Please cut along ▬▬▬▬ for your child.

dachshund

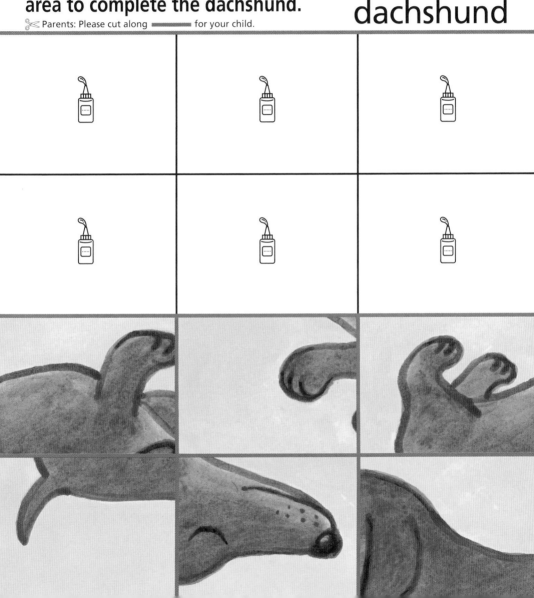

39

Spotted Snake

To parents

This is the last exercise in this workbook. Compare your child's work on this exercise with his or her earlier work. You will probably notice a lot of progress in your child's ability to arrange and paste parts correctly. Offer lots of praise for his or her accomplishment!

Paste the cut out parts onto the white area to complete the snake.

✂ Parents: Please cut along ▬▬▬ for your child.

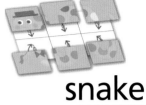

snake

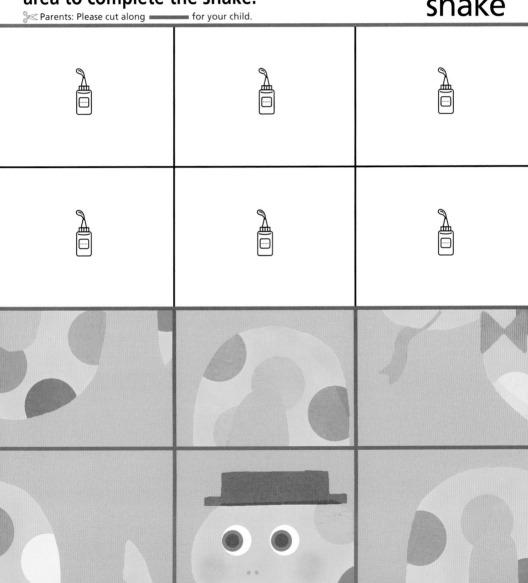

KUM◯N

Certificate of Achievement

_____

is hereby congratulated on completing

Let's Sticker & Paste! Amazing Animals

Presented on _____ , 20 _____

_____
Parent or Guardian